This book belongs to:

____

Made in the USA
Las Vegas, NV
07 December 2023

82298516R00061